Road Map To Wealth
By
Bruce Roth

This is a book that is intended to be a companion to our web seminar by the same name. Our intention is to help our clients and readers to accomplish the elusive goal of financial independence. This is defined in the body of the book but I will define it here as well.

Financial independence means having enough income producing assets that give off enough income so that you can live comfortably for the rest of your life. If living comfortably would use up the assets before the end of your life, that is not financial independence.

We have used some ideas from other sources and have given them credit where appropriate.

If you would like to explore the ideas contained in this book in greater detail and see how they would apply to your particular situation, please contact me at (702) 277-1303 or write to me at LasVegasBruce@gmail.com or 8079 Pinnacle Peak Avenue Las Vegas, NV 89113.

This book is taken from a presentation I gave to two employees of a local Mortgage Company as a way of introducing them to the material. I hope you find it interesting and informative. I did have their permission to record the conversation.

The Secret Of The Rich

Bruce I didn't catch the name of the other Loan Officer you have on the line. I apologize. What's your name again?

Thank you for taking the time to come and experience this. I hope it will add a lot of value to you. Nothing I'm going to say here is new to the world and it's just kind of a way of looking at it in a concise order. You can see on my screen here that we're starting with The Secret of the Rich. We can call this Roadmap to Wealth or The Secret of the Rich. The lawyers require me to read this to you. I apologize. I know it's boring and long, please bear with me this roadmap is just one of many ways of how one can become a millionaire starting with very little investment. There's absolutely no guarantee that one will achieve the results contemplated by this roadmap because each person's situation is unique. Your result may be better or may be worst. Bruce Roth and Keller Williams Realty Southwest assume absolutely no responsibility for any adverse results from following this roadmap. The first thing I'm going to do is talk a little bit about the difference between the wealthy and the rest of the people. When I say "you", I mean middle class and poor. Please don't take personal offense if you live more like the wealthy. This is for the average American. The difference between you and them is they have a plan to become financially independent. You have a plan to go on vacation.

What Is The Difference Between You & Them

Them

Have a plan to become financially independent

You

Have a plan to go on vacation

Another difference between you and them is they use tax loopholes and you do not. A lot of people, even people who own a house, don't even itemize on their taxes.

A difference between you and them is they own assets and you own debts.

What Is The Difference Between You & Them

Them

Own Assets

You

Own Debts

Here are some of the problems from not having a plan: 46% of all American workers have less than $10,000 in savings, according to the Employee Benefits Research Institute. They also say that 29% of American workers have less than $1000 in savings. And startlingly they also say that 25% of Americans have $0 in savings. I find this to be a little scary.

Back in 1991, half of all American workers planned to retire before they reach the age of 65. Today the number of people who plan to retire by age 65 has plunged to just 23%. And these numbers are 2008 numbers.

I would bet that number is much lower than 23% by now because of the downturn in the economy.

Results Of Not Having A Plan

46% of all American workers have less than $10,000 in savings.
Employee Benefits Research Institute

29% of all American workers have less than $1,000 in savings.
Employee Benefits Research Institute

Back in 1991, half of all American workers planned to retire before they reached the age of 65. Today, that number has plunged to just 23%.

USA Today says that Americans' greatest fear is running out of money. Do you have a fear of running out of money before you die?

American's greatest fear is running out of money!

This is something I borrowed from Rich Dad Poor Dad. It's the game of money, and the object of this game is to put aside enough assets that you can be financially independent as early in the game as possible. The way we define financially independent is having enough income producing assets that are giving off enough income that you can choose not go to work if you don't want to. You'll work because you want to, not because you have to.

The Game Of Money

Courtesy of
Robert Kiyosaki
Author of Rich Dad
Poor Dad

The first part is the pregame show. That's going to school or when you were a child. Most people enter the workforce really in a serious way at about age 25, so most people work for about 40 years or at least that's the plan in this country. We call 25-35 the first quarter. The idea here, again, is to put aside enough assets to be financially independent.

The Game Of Money

Courtesy of
Robert Kiyosaki
Author of Rich Dad
Poor Dad

Most people make almost no progress in the first quarter. Most are not earning very much This is the time many people get married and buy a house, and they end up having debts. They're going backwards rather than forwards towards being financially independent. In the second quarter, maybe their income has gone up a little bit but most times their debts have also gone up a little bit. Most of their debts have gone up equally or in a greater measure. Most people do nothing to reach the goal of financial independence.

The Game Of Money

During halftime, ages at about age 45 is a time when couples will divorce or make a purchase that they really cannot afford. Maybe a boat or a sport car, and this will set them back instead of help move them forward.

The Game Of Money

25-35	First Quarter
35-45	Second Quarter
	Half Time
45-55	Third Quarter

In the third quarter, 45-55, this is when most people start taking significant money off the table. Their skills have gotten much better and they're probably at or near the peak of their earning capacity. And if they're playing their cards right, they're scooping it up and buying assets left and right. Unfortunately, because they didn't start when they were younger, the money is going to have less time to accumulate and the truth is that 95% of Americans will never achieve it, even by the end of the fourth quarter at age 65, which is very, very sad to me.

The Game Of Money

Pre-game Show

25-35	First Quarter
35-45	Second Quarter
	Half Time
45-55	Third Quarter
55-65	Fourth Quarter

Courtesy of
Robert Kiyosaki
Author of Rich Dad
Poor Dad

What happens if they haven't put enough aside to be financially independent by 65, they end up in overtime. And if you have to be working in overtime, many people find themselves learning new phrases and meeting interesting people, and learning new phrase like "Welcome to Wal-Mart." And the truly sad thing is so many people don't even do it in this time. They don't become financially independent and they find themselves, as sad as it may be, out of time.

The Game Of Money

Pre-game Show

25-35	First Quarter
35-45	Second Quarter
	Half Time
45-55	Third Quarter
55-65	Fourth Quarter
	Over Time
	Out of Time

Courtesy of
Robert Kiyosaki
Author of Rich Dad
Poor Dad

We're going to try and help you figure out how to get there before you hit the end of the game.

There are really only four ways to get significant amounts of money. The first way, the old fashion way is to marry it. I don't know about you but I'm married and this way is not available to me because I'm already married. Another way is to inherit it and the third way is to invent something.

The truth is this is the way that most people these days who become super wealthy are getting there. 30 years ago, when I looked at Forbes Fortune 400, almost all the people there had most of their money in real estate and almost all of them had made most of their money in real estate, which is why I became a Real Estate Broker all those years ago. But in the last 30 years we've had the tech revolution and a lot of the people who are at the top of the money pyramid have either invented something like Bill Gates or Apple, or Google, one of those companies, or they're one of those Hedge Fund managers where they're just raking it off.

Ways To Get Money

Marry It!

Inherit It!

Invent Something!

Save It!

The truth is that probably the only way that's available to you and I is to save it. There's this great book about this called The Millionaire Next Door.

The book was written by people who went and interviewed all these millionaires. There's something like 3-4 million millionaires in the United States. What they found out is that our society's conception of what a millionaire is and who they are is inaccurate and doesn't compute with what they found. They found that most of the people who are millionaires in America, are professional; either they're educated or they own their small business. They worked hard, they have a good income and they banked a lot of it and bought assets that were appreciating. They invested in the stock market and they bought real estate. Real estate was the most common things amongst these three million millionaires that they looked at. And that's the only real way that's available to me or most people. When most people think about routes to financial independent, they think about these first few ways; the stock market, the money market, mutual funds and savings account. All of those are perfectly good vehicles and I recommend that you use them, but the problem with them is that they just don't have the rate of return that real estate does.

ROUTES to Financial Independence

- Stock Market
- Money Market
- Mutual Funds
- Savings Accounts
- **Real Estate**

To be a great real estate investor, you need to understand these three principles: the power of compounding, the power of leverage and the power of staying the course. I'm going to explain each of these in some detail right now.

KEYS to Real Estate Investment

- Power of Compounding
- Power of Leverage
- Power of Staying the Course

I will explain each one of these in detail

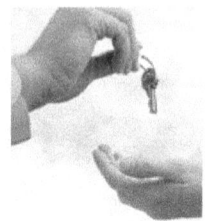

Here's a great quote I love from Albert Einstein, "The magic of compounding interest is the greatest discovery of the 20th century." This is a guy who is known because he discovered relativity and he says that compounding interest is the greatest discover of the 20th century.

The magic of compounding interest is the greatest discovery of the 20th century!

Albert Einstein

Take a look at the chart below. Let's pretend that you and a friend of yours are both 24 years old and you decide you want to try and put a little money aside for retirement. You go out and find an account that pays 6% interest compounding annually. And your friend gets serious about putting money in and puts in $2000 a year every year for 10 years. You on the other hand fall asleep at the switch and don't do anything for 10 years then you start putting $2000 a year away until age 65. Your friend stopped at age 34, so you're putting 2 ½ times as much money in the account as your friend, but even though the money is accumulating interest, he ends up with $171,000 and you end up with $182,000. And the reason this is important is because by starting earlier, you get a jump on the game and you can really take advantage of the time element and compounding interest. Another important point from this chart is if your friend had stuck to it, he'd have a lot more money. It's important to get started early and stick to it.

If a person is more mature and they think there is not enough time for the compounding effect to take place, they can put money aside for their children or even grandchildren. By buying a property when your grandchild is born, there is a good chance that the property and any others you buy for the same reason will pay for them to go to college and even make every problem in their life easier to manage.

UNDENIABLE Power of Leverage

- Common misconception:
  - "My Home is the best investment I ever made!"
  - If you bought your home in 1990 for $250,000 and sold it in June of 2003 for $600,000 that is a gain of 140%.
  - During the same period, the Dow Jones grew from 2590 to 9188. That is a gain of 255%.
- REALITY
  - It is the FINANCING of your home that was the best investment decision you ever made.
  - In 1990, you put down $50,000 for the purchase of a $250,000 house. This $50,000 cash investment produced a profit of $350,000 or a total return of 600%. 600% is far greater than the 255% earned by the stock market.

The next point is leverage. Leverage is really one of the most powerful principles out there and I'm going to give the same example twice. I'm sure you've heard this, you may have even said this, "My home is the best investment I've ever made."

Let's say you bought a home in 1990 for $250,000 and in 2003 you sold that property again for $600,000. That's 13 years later. You'd have a gain of 140%, so that's a little over 10% a year. That's not bad. It's not great but it's not bad, certainly better than that 6% we were talking about a minute ago. The Dow, during that same time, went from 2590 to 9188, and that's a gain of 255%. So most people look at that and they go "wow, I should have my money in the market instead of real estate" but that's not taking into account leverage.

No one would pay cash for the house in real estate and leverage is something that really is only available to you in real estate, not in any other investment vehicle. You'd put $50,000 down on the property, get a $200,000 loan, again you sell it for the same $600,000, you'd have a gain of $350,000 or a total return of 600%, rather than the 255% and that's not even taking into account any rents you might accumulate that might exceed the mortgage payments or tax advantages. There's a lot of money here in the real estate and that's the power of leverage, which can make investing in real estate more powerful than any of the other vehicles.

The next principle is the power of time and staying the course.

Here's a mistake that's all too common. I'm sure you've seen it. Someone will buy a house, a starter home, when they're young. Maybe they don't have any kids yet or they are just starting a family. It might not be in a great neighborhood, maybe a really small house, but at least they get into something and it starts appreciating.

Now 5-7 years later, maybe they're making a little more money, there's another child or two, they need to be where there's a better school, so they trade up to a nicer, more expensive house. But they sell the first house in order to buy the second house. They buy that second house and then they live there for 5-7 years. Now they're doing very well financially, so they buy a villa and they stay in that house. They sell the second house in order to buy the big nice house. And they stay in that house for some period of time 5, 7, or even 10 years and then the kids are gone. Maybe they're tired of yard work, they're tired of having a pool, so they sell the big house and they buy a condo or a small house, maybe in a senior retirement community, something like that. And it seems good at that time, each time they did that, but the problem is that they lose the power of staying the course, the compounding.

I will show you with an excel spreadsheet how the longer you hold on to a property, the greater your average rate of appreciation is, even using the same appreciation percent on the total value of the property. Getting rid of the property is like shooting yourself in the foot over and over again.

The next one I want to talk about is just five year increments of what property appreciation has done nationwide.. Using California as an example, for the last 5 years, California has gone up by 16% average per year, nationwide average 7% per year. over the last 44 years, California has gone up an average of 6.9% year after year after year. Nationwide values have gone up an average of 5% per year.

PERCENTAGE of Property Value Appreciation

YEAR	CALIFORNIA	NATIONWIDE
Last 5 yrs.	16%	7%
Last 10 yrs.	9%	6%
Last 15 yrs.	6%	5%
Last 20 yrs.	7%	5%
Last 25 yrs.	7%	5%
Last 30 yrs.	9%	6%
Last 35 yrs.	9%	6%
Last 44 yrs.	6.9%	5%

Bruce: Over the last 44 years, we're looking at rates of appreciation of 6.9% in California or 5% in the country. Here's an example that we made up just to give you an idea of what 5% appreciation per year can do over 21 years in this example. Let's say you bought a house today for $210,000. Got an FHA loan, you put 3.5% down. I put 4.5% for the interest rate, even though rates are probably under 4% now. That would be $13,382.17 to get into the property. The property is worth $210,000, it appreciates at 5% per year for 21 years so the value at that time is going to be $585,052.14. The mortgage has been paid down from the $206,196.38 to $93,335.69 over that period of time. So you have an equity position 21 years from now that's gone from $13,382 to $491,716.45. If you only take the cash position, that's the return. See how there's the equity position, there's your investment, there's the total return. There it is as a percent, 3574% or an annual rate of 170%. But that doesn't take into account the tax advantages of having owned that property, which means you're going to have a $195% average annual rate of return on your $13,000 investment. Imagine going to a financial planner and telling them that you wanted that kind of return, what do you think their response would be?

They'd laugh at you, I think. But that's a spectacular rate of return. Is there anything about those numbers that you think is unrealistic or I'm blowing smoke? I'm sorry, I didn't hear you.

Richard: I've seen the numbers. It makes sense.

Bruce: The question is, "How do you become a savvy real estate investor?" That's where I come in. Our job is to be your real estate investment consultants, hopefully for life, and our role is to help our clients to develop a plan and execute it to maximize balance, safety, rate of return and tax advantage, because we think it's really important to take advantage of all those things.

Here's the $64 question for you, *'Are you ready to become a millionaire?'*

Well it's pretty simple and I think I'm going to use conservative numbers. Let's take a look here at this spreadsheet. Let's start with property #1. Your plan may vary from this, but this is an example. We are going to assume that you are a first time home buyer. If you own one or more now, that would shift.

Let's say you buy a property for $210,000 with a 3.5% down payment, FHA. It requires $13,382.17 to get into the property.

You hold on to the property for 7 years. You get an average rate of return of 5% average so you have about $115,000 in equity 7 years from now and your annual rate of return, not counting tax benefits, is 109% but using the tax benefits, 138%. Now I want you to remember that, 138%, because we're going to come back here in a minute.

We're going to talk about why you need to hold on to the property.

Now let's say after those 7 years you decide to buy another property for $375,000. Again you're going to be an owner-occupant. You're going to rent out the first property and you're going to put 3.5% down for FHA, so you have to come up with just under $22,000. Here's an important question for you. In those 7 years, do you think you're going to be able to save that $22,000?

If after 7 years you have $110,000 equity in it as the spreadsheet shows us you will, you can borrow against the equity from the first property to get the down payment on the second property. This may create a slightly higher debt service but it is well within the range of what is workable ad makes sense.

The way that you will have this much equity in the property is that with the property appreciating by 5% per year, which gives you a value of $295,491. The $206,196 loan amount has now been paid down over 7 years to $179,815.50 and if you subtract them, that's the number you get. You follow me? Are we good to go on that? Let me ask you this, do you think the 5% annual appreciation is reasonable for us to expect over the next 7 years?

Down Payment	$7,350.00
Closing Costs	$6,032.17
Total Investment	**$13,382.17**

Equity At Time Of Rental

Current Value	$210,000.00
Appreciation Rate	5.00%
Years Until Time of Rental	7
Estimated Value at Time of Rental	$295,491.09
1st TD Loan Balance At Time of Rental	$179,815.50
2nd TD Loan Balance at Time of Rental	$0.00
Equity Position at Time of Rental	**$115,675.59**

Return on Investment

Equity Position at Time of Rental	$115,675.59
Total Investment	$13,382.17
Total Return	$102,293.41
Total Return %	764.40%
Annual Rate of Return	109.20%

Return on Investment after Tax Savings

Interest Paid upto Time of Rental	$61,379.53
RE Taxes Paid upto Time of Rental	$16,170.00
Total Deduction	$77,549.53
Personal Income Tax Rate	35.00%
Tax Savings	$27,142.34
Return berfore Tax Savings	$102,293.41
Total Return on Investment with Tax Savings	$129,435.75
Total Return with Tax Savings %	**967.23%**
Annual Rate of Return %	**138.18%**
Down Payment	$13,125.00

Closing Costs	$8,467.94
Total Investment	**$21,592.94**

Equity At Time Of Rental

Current Value	$375,000.00
Appreciation Rate	5.00%
Years Until Time of Rental	7
Estimated Value at Time of Rental	$527,662.66
1st TD Loan Balance At Time of Rental	$330,613.75
2nd TD Loan Balance at Time of Rental	
Equity Position at Time of Rental	**$197,048.91**

Return on Investment

Equity Position at Time of Rental	$197,048.91
Total Investment	$21,592.94
Total Return	$175,455.97
Total Return %	812.56%
Annual Rate of Return	116.08%

Return on Investment after Tax Savings

Interest Paid upto Time of Rental	$147,843.65
RE Taxes Paid upto Time of Rental	$28,875.00
Total Deduction	$176,718.65
Personal Income Tax Rate	35.00%
Tax Savings	$61,851.53
Return berfore Tax Savings	$175,455.97
Total Return on Investment with Tax Savings	$237,307.50
Total Return with Tax Savings %	**1099.01%**
Annual Rate of Return %	**157.00%**

Equity Availabe at Time of Rental

LTV at time of Rental	62.66%
Equity Available for HELOC up to 75%	$65,133.25
Down Payment	$7,350.00
Closing Costs	$6,032.17
Total Investment	**$13,382.17**

Equity At Time Of Rental

Current Value	$210,000.00
Appreciation Rate	5.00%
Years Until Time of Rental	14
Estimated Value at Time of Rental	$415,785.64
1st TD Loan Balance At Time of Rental	$143,317.70
2nd TD Loan Balance at Time of Rental	$0.00
Equity Position at Time of Rental	**$272,467.94**

Return on Investment

Equity Position at Time of Rental	$272,467.94
Total Investment	$13,382.17
Total Return	$259,085.77
Total Return %	1936.05%
Annual Rate of Return	138.29%

Return on Investment after Tax Savings

Interest Paid up to Time of Rental	$112,642.13
RE Taxes Paid up to Time of Rental	$32,340.00
Total Deduction	$144,982.13
Personal Income Tax Rate	35.00%
Tax Savings	$50,743.75
Return before Tax Savings	$259,085.77
Total Return on Investment with Tax Savings	$309,829.51
Total Return with Tax Savings %	**2315.24%**
Annual Rate of Return %	**165.37%**

Equity Availabe at Time of Rental

LTV at time of Rental	34.47%
Equity Available for HELOC up to 75%	$168,521.53

So if you'll notice, your annual rate of return after your taxes is now 165% just on the first property. That's going to change again in one minute when we do the third property. Now let's say you go to buy the third property. You want to buy a $500,000.00 house at that point. Again, let's say FHA limits have gone up. You buy it with an FHA loan. We have no idea what interest rates are going to be so I just stuck a number in there. It doesn't really mean much anyway, because one of the things I do for my clients is we're going to reevaluate this every year, year and half, maybe two years, depending on your situation to see if it's time to try and buy another property or maybe trade your equity into another property using a 1031 exchange.

Under the 1031 provision of the Internal Revenue Code, you can sell like-kind property, reinvest the profits into the new property without having to be taxed capital gains in between, so you could take the equity from the first property, put it into a second or third or fourth property or you can take the equity from two or three properties and put it into one big property. That way you don't get taxed on it. And if you never sell it, other than through a 1031, you'll never be taxed on it and your estate won't be taxed because if you do it right, your heirs can probably inherit tax free.

But that's a story that we're going to have to bring a CPA in to discuss in detail. So you buy a property for $500,000.00. You put $27,817.87 for total cost to close. Again, you hold on to it for 7 years. It appreciates at 5%. It's now worth $703,000.00 and your first loan is now paid down to $444,000 and change. This is making no additional payments on any of these mortgages.

You have $258,962.00 in equity in property #3. Property #2 you've now owned this one for 14 years, so you have $469,572.00 in equity. And property #1, you've now owned it for 21 years, so you have $491,716.45 in equity. Between the three properties: $491,000 + $469,000 + $258,000 is over $1.2 million. Are you with me? That's how you become a millionaire in 21 years. That's a million dollars in your estate, over and above what you would otherwise have if you don't do this.

Down Payment	$7,350.00
Closing Costs	$6,032.17
Total Investment	**$13,382.17**

Equity At Time Of Rental

Current Value	$210,000.00
Appreciation Rate	5.00%
Years Until Time of Rental	21
Estimated Value at Time of Rental	$585,052.14
1st TD Loan Balance At Time of Rental	$93,335.69
2nd TD Loan Balance at Time of Rental	$0.00
Equity Position at Time of Rental	**$491,716.45**

Return on Investment

Equity Position at Time of Rental	$491,716.45
Total Investment	$13,382.17
Total Return	$478,334.28
Total Return %	3574.41%
Annual Rate of Return	170.21%

Return on Investment after Tax Savings

Interest Paid up to Time of Rental	$150,420.54
RE Taxes Paid up to Time of Rental	$48,510.00
Total Deduction	$198,930.54
Personal Income Tax Rate	35.00%
Tax Savings	$69,625.69
Return berfore Tax Savings	$478,334.28
Total Return on Investment with Tax Savings	$547,959.96
Total Return with Tax Savings %	**4094.70%**
Annual Rate of Return %	**194.99%**

Equity Available at Time of Rental

LTV at time of Rental	15.95%
Equity Available for HELOC up to 75%	$345,453.41
Down Payment	$13,125.00
Closing Costs	$8,467.94
Total Investment	**$21,592.94**

Equity At Time Of Rental

Current Value	$375,000.00
Appreciation Rate	5.00%
Years Until Time of Rental	14
Estimated Value at Time of Rental	$742,474.35
1st TD Loan Balance At Time of Rental	$272,902.34
2nd TD Loan Balance at Time of Rental	
Equity Position at Time of Rental	**$469,572.01**

Return on Investment

Equity Position at Time of Rental	$469,572.01
Total Investment	$21,592.94
Total Return	$447,979.07
Total Return %	2074.66%
Annual Rate of Return	148.19%

Return on Investment after Tax Savings

Interest Paid up to Time of Rental	$275,569.97
RE Taxes Paid up to Time of Rental	$57,750.00
Total Deduction	$333,319.97
Personal Income Tax Rate	35.00%
Tax Savings	$116,661.99
Return before Tax Savings	$447,979.07

Total Return on Investment with Tax Savings	$564,641.05
Total Return with Tax Savings %	**2614.93%**
Annual Rate of Return %	**186.78%**
Down Payment	$17,500.00
Closing Costs	$10,317.87
Total Investment	**$27,817.87**

Equity At Time Of Rental

Current Value	$500,000.00
Appreciation Rate	5.00%
Years Until Time of Rental	7
Estimated Value at Time of Rental	$703,550.21
1st TD Loan Balance At Time of Rental	$444,587.82
2nd TD Loan Balance at Time of Rental	
Equity Position at Time of Rental	**$258,962.39**

Return on Investment

Equity Position at Time of Rental	$258,962.39
Total Investment	$27,817.87
Total Return	$231,144.53
Total Return %	830.92%
Annual Rate of Return	118.70%

Return on Investment after Tax Savings

Interest Paid upto Time of Rental	$214,304.34
RE Taxes Paid upto Time of Rental	$38,500.00
Total Deduction	$252,804.34
Personal Income Tax Rate	35.00%
Tax Savings	$88,481.52
Return berfore Tax Savings	$231,144.53

Total Return on Investment with Tax Savings	$319,626.05
Total Return with Tax Savings %	**1149.00%**
Annual Rate of Return %	**164.14%**

Equity Available at Time of Rental

LTV at time of Rental	63.19%
Equity Available for HELOC up to 75%	$83,074.84

At this point, if you are young enough you may decide to keep going and do this another time, another time, another time. Or if you want to cash out early, let's say you sold this property. You took the $258,000 and you paid off most of this mortgage. You're going to have like $18,000.00, $19,000.00, $20,000.00 left on it. And then you have this property, the first one, $93,000.00 mortgage on it. The second one has no mortgage on it and whatever you can rent that it's throwing off good cash flow and you have this one, you're living in it with a very low mortgage.

When my parents first bought the house that I grew up in, they had a mortgage payment of $135 a month. They thought they were going to choke on the mortgage because $135 seemed too much to pay. 24 years later when they were about ready to pay it off, because it was a 24 year 6 month mortgage, they thought that $135 a month was nickels and that's going to be true for you too.

If you buy a house today, 21 years from now it's going to seem like nickels, whatever your payment is. But notice that your annual rate of return on property #1, which was in the

130% the first time, then 160%, is now 195%. That's why it's important to hold these properties and not just sell them because you get the much higher rates of return over the latter years of owning it.

Here's another thing I want to explain. I'm going to go with $1.2 million, just the equity in these properties, not counting any rent that exceeds your payments or anything like that, just the equity. Not even the tax benefits. If you take $1.2 million and divide that by 21 years, that means you earn an average of $57,000.00 a year over those 21 years, just from owning these three properties, not from going to work every day, not counting what you can earn, originating loans or whatever you're doing later on. The question becomes, here's the real $64 question, "How many times do you think you should do this in your life?"

While you can afford it, obviously you want to buy as many houses as you can. Just in case you are worried about how you can afford to pay all three mortgages, you're not going to be paying three mortgages. The tenants are going to be paying two of them for you. If you do your homework is that right now you will find that on a new purchase your principal, interest, taxes and insurance, not counting your tax benefits, is going to be almost exactly what you're paying on that house renting it. You could buy the one next door for the same payment.

Many people worry that they won't know how to find good tenants. In my market and for my clients I'll be glad and grateful to help them find tenants. I'll only charge them half a months' rent to do it. And I'm not going to do the management. If they want management, I have a manager that I'll refer them to.

That's the story here. You save a little money, you buy property, and there are also tricks that I have that you guys may be unaware of, to help them avoid having tenant problems. One trick that I have is let's just, for conversation sake, the rent on a property is $2100. Just for conversation's sake. I know that's kind of a high rent here in Las Vegas but let's just use it for an example. You advertise it at $2100. You get 2 or 3 tenants interested. You pick the tenant you want and I'll do the background check for them and everything. You run the credit, you do the whole thing, and you go to the tenant and you say "I really, really, really, really want you never to call me in the middle of the night to fix your toilet. I want you to handle everything. Every month that you don't call me, I'll deduct $50 from the rent and every month that the letter that you send the check in is postmarked on the first of the month or earlier, I'll give you another $50 off the rent, so you only owe me $2000. You pay me early and you leave me alone, I'll give you $100 discount."

That's something that me as the landlord, or me as the real estate broker and the landlord in unison are going to offer to the tenant. That way the tenant won't bug the hell out of this landlord who doesn't know how to manage a property. That's the same $100 that they'd have to pay a property manager to do the job for them. There are a lot of things I can do to help them.

Thank you for taking the time to read this book. It is a transcription of a phone presentation I did in November of 2014. If you would like to discuss how these principles might apply to the specifics of your situation, please call me at (702) 277-1303 or write me at LasVegasBruce@gmail.com.

If you live or want to buy or sell Real Property in some area outside of my main service areas, I would be glad to help make sure that you find an honest Real Estate professional to work with. I am part of a referral network that is all over North America and much of the rest of the world.